YOU'LL NEVER WALK ALO

David Orme lives in W̶̶̶̶̶ ̶̶̶̶̶ty. He
has written ̶̶̶̶̶̶̶̶̶̶̶̶̶̶ cture
books for ̶̶̶̶̶̶̶̶̶̶ends ̶ ̶̶̶̶̶̶ his time
in schools performing and writing poetry, and encouraging
children and teachers to take an active interest in poetry.

Marc Vyvyan-Jones has a studio in the Bristol Craft Centre,
where he is surrounded by other free-spirited artists. He
trained as an architect, which wasn't the right life for him, so
he ran away to become an illustrator and morris dancer.

earwig-o, earwig-o, earwig-o!

YOU'LL NEVER WALK ALONE

MORE FOOTBALL POEMS

chosen by
David Orme

and illustrated by

Marc Vyvyan-Jones

MACMILLAN
CHILDREN'S BOOKS

First published 1995 by
Macmillan Children's Books
a division of Macmillan Publishers Ltd
25 Eccleston Place, London SW1W 9NF
and Basingstoke

Associated companies throughout the world

ISBN 0 330 33787 4

9 8 7 6 5 4 3 2

A CIP catalogue record for this book is
available from the British Library.

The publishers would like to thank Rogers, Coleridge &
White Ltd for permission to reproduce 'Tell Me About
Your Dream' by Gareth Owen (© Gareth Owen 1995).

earwig-o, earwig-o, earwig-o!

Contents

Extra Time: Football Facts

Worm's-Eye-View of
the Replay at Wembley

What's that pattering?
Can it be rain?
Oh no – a re-play!
'Ere we go again . . .

Tony Mitton
Manchester United

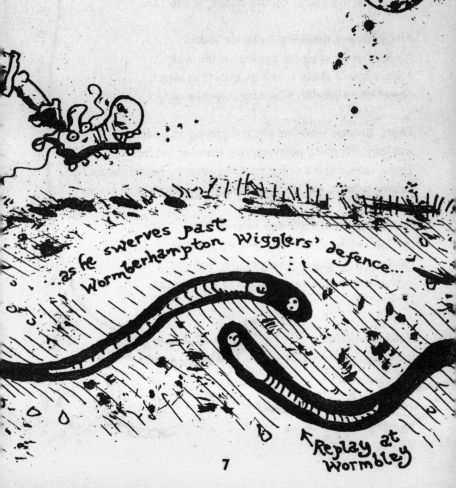

. . . as he swerves past Wormberhampton Wigglers' defence . . .

Replay at Wormbley

Catch of the Day's Shoal of the Season

Always choose an octopus for goalie
Always have a whale for the defensive wall
Always have a salmon for high crosses
Never let a swordfish head the ball at all.

Never make an enemy of a sea anemone
Never have a clash with a giant clam
Never pull a mussel in a tackle or a tussle
Always let the kipper be the skipper if you can.

Always have a mackerel to tackle well
Always have a sting-ray staying on the wing
Always have a shark – he's an expert at attack
Never kiss a jellyfish who scores with a sting.

There are eels who feel electric playing at a pace that's hectic
and lobster's going potty scoring from an indirect kick.
There are dolphins doing dribbling weaving round shoals,
helping whelks, out-thinking winkles, getting lots of goals.

Mediterranean, Pacific and Atlantic
the football is specific yet very very frantic.
Millions of matches of varying degrees
in the twenty thousand leagues under the seas.

Paul Cookson
Everton

can I 'av
me ball
back?

Goal!

An excitement spark
A net bulger
A keep distresser
A seat spring
A defender incenser
A manager's grin-maker
A trainer jumper
A scoreboard changer
A crowd maddener
A glory glory spreader
A team promoter
A game finisher
A fun-journey-home-maker.

Daniel Sedgwick
Ipswich Town

We Cannot Lose Again!

Here we go and here we go
and here we go again
hoping that today our brilliant team
will reach its peak.
Last Saturday was dreadful,
our defence just looked so weak,
but now it's our turn to be lucky,
for we cannot lose again!

Here we go and here we go
and here we go again –
we cannot get the stupid ball
stuck into their net
and they're looking deadly
when they break out quickly, yet
it's our turn to be lucky,
for we cannot lose again!
Here we go and here we go

we're a load of rubbish!....

you only sing when you're winning!

useless united

and here we go again
wishing we'd gone and done
some shopping in the town,
but we mustn't give up easily,
we're only one goal down
and it's our turn to be lucky,
for we cannot lose again!

Here we go and here we go
and here we go again
leaving after losing,
our position's looking bleak.
Yet all of us will congregate
to cheer them on next week
when it's our turn to be lucky,
for we cannot lose again!

Peter Comaish
Liverpool

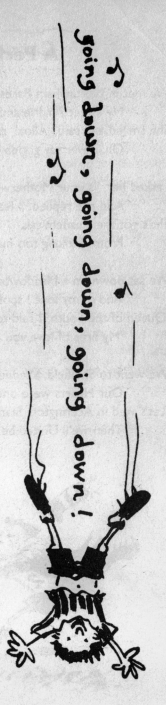

going down, going down, going down, going down!

A Perfect Match

We met in Nottingham Forest,
My sweet Airdrie and I.
She smiled and said, 'Alloa!' to me –
Oh, never say goodbye!

I asked her, 'Is your Motherwell?'
And she replied, 'I fear
She's got the Academicals
From drinking too much beer.'

We sat down on a Meadowbank
And of my love I spoke.
'Queen of the South,' I said to her,
'My fires of love you Stoke!'

We went to Sheffield, Wednesday.
Our Hearts were one. Said she:
'Let's wed in Accrington, Stanley,
Then we'll United be.'

The ring was Stirling silver,
     Our friends, Forfar and wide,
A motley Crewe, all gathered there
     and fought to kiss the bride.

The best man had an awful lisp.
     'Come Raith your glatheth up,'
He said, and each man raised on high
     His Coca-Cola cup.

The honeymoon was spent abroad:
     We flew out east by Ayr,
And found the far-off Orient
     Partick-ularly fair.

We're home, in our own Villa now,
     (The Walsall painted grey)
And on our Chesterfield we sit
     And watch Match of the Day.

Pam Gidney
Chelsea

Just Signed

13

Tell Me About Your Dream

'Well
It's always the same you see
Never varies
And always leaves me sweating with fright.
Talk you through it?
Well, I'll try.

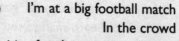

I'm at a big football match
In the crowd
And we're all waiting for the teams to emerge
When suddenly over the speakers
This voice comes
Very loud and very clear
And I get the feeling
It's speaking to me.

Do I remember what it says?
Well yes:
Two players have missed the coach
So they're a man short.
If anybody happens
To have their boots on them
They'd be grateful if he'd play.
What?
Of course I've got my boots
Because I know from my dream
That this may happen.
That's right
I don't know if it's a dream or not.
In a flash
I'm over the barrier
And in the dressing-rooms.
Suddenly famous players
Are shaking my hand

14

And clapping me on the back.
As we set off down the tunnel
The manager puts his hand on my arm.
He looks me in the eye and says,
"Take the number 9 shirt lad
Wear it with pride lad
You're captain for the day."

And then I'm off
Up the dark tunnel
To a green field called Glory.
My studs rattle on the concrete
And the roar of the crowd
Is like a great beast breathing
Far away.
Breathing my name over and over.
I come to a wall.

I don't know whether to go left or right.
I take the right one
But the right one
Turns out to be the wrong one.
It leads to another corridor
And another
And another
And another.
The beast has stopped breathing now
I call out
But my voice
Comes back off the endless white walls.

Then I wake up
Sweating and shaking with fright.
Well that's it.
Has it helped to talk about it?
Well, yes I suppose it has.
Do I want to ask any questions?

Well there is one thing.
I don't know if you can tell me
But
Is this a dream?'

Gareth Owen
Everton

perhaps you are in my dream.

Miracles Can Happen

Dad stomped in, all grumpy and sore,
He stamped his feet and slammed the door.
He growled and grimaced and threw down his coat,
And made funny noises down in his throat.
Then Mum said kindly, 'Don't worry dear –
United might still win a game this year . . .'

Samson United

They're the strongest team in the league –
Not because they're the best,
But because they're stuck at the bottom
And have to prop up the rest . . .

Dead Cert

After missing his umpteenth penalty,
'I could kick myself,' he said.
'I wouldn't bother, you'd only miss,'
Muttered poor old manager Fred.

Clive Webster
Sheffield United

17

Wilmington Wanderers' Weekly Wash

Eleven shirts, eleven shorts, twenty-one socks . . .
Twenty-one socks? Where's the one that got away?
Eleven shirts, eleven shorts, twenty-TWO socks
Went whirling round in the washer window.

I'll have to find a substitute – a transfer from the Cubs?
It's not exactly 'Strip' I know, but with a bit of luck,
Nobody'll notice the lack of navy stripes.

Eleven shirts, eleven shorts, twenty-TWO socks
Whirled round that washer window.
The power-packed powder pounded the stains
(The packet said it removed the most stubborn).
Perhaps that sock was all dirt!

Catherine Benson
Wilmington Wanderers and
Bradford City

1..2..3...4...5..

...Feed the machine more socks!

Nightplayer

My dad's mad about football.
He even plays it in his dreams.
My mum doesn't mind that much,
But the whistle makes her scream.

Janis Priestley
Aston Villa

19

Football on the Brain

In the yard at ten to nine.
In the yard at break.
On the field at dinner-time
until our legs all ache.

Out there when it's cold and hard.
Out there in the rain.
That's the way with our lot:
Football on the brain.

Some like playing marbles.
Some like games of chase.
Some just like to muck about
and stand around the place.

But our lot run together
with passes swift and neat.
Out lot's always on the move,
a football at our feet.

Some say, 'I'd get tired.'
Some say, 'I'd get bored.'
But they don't know the buzz you get
when you're the one that's scored.

Some say, 'Why the trouble?'
Some say, 'What's the fuss?'
But our lot's off to Wembley.
That's the place for us.

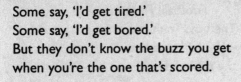

Out there when it's cold and hard.
Out there in the rain.
That's the way with our lot:
Football on the brain.

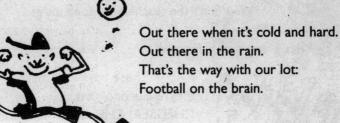

Tony Mitton
Manchester United

he's got
football
on the
....brain!

21

Football!

Football! *Football!*
The boys want the *entire* playground
and we're left squashed
against the broken fence.
Why don't the teachers stop them?
Why?
Haven't they got *any* sense?

My friend Anna
ran across the tarmac.

Smack!
Got the football right on her nose.
Blood all over her face.
Why don't the teachers do something?
Why?
It's a disgrace, a disgrace!

Those boys . . . I mean
they're like hooligans.
CHEL-SEA! CHEL-SEA! they chant
morning, noon and night.
The teacher on duty does . . . nothing.
Why?
It's just . . . it's just not right!

We complain bitterly
but the duty teacher says,
'Go and see the Head. He's in charge.'
Him! He's *useless!* YOU-ESS-LESS!
When we ask him to ban football
why,
oh why, can't he just say 'Yes'?

Wes Magee
Swindon Town

22

Out of the Cup

An open goal, lad, a gaping, can't-miss goal!
A banged-in, dead-cert, asking-for-it goal!
Talk about butter-fingers – we'll have to call you
butter-boots! What d'you do? Smear Kerrygold on them?

All you had to do was tap it in, a simple tap,
a toe-cap tap. But no! you had to dash at it,
to rush at it, to take a mighty swipe at it.
I'm not the only one

who wished to hear a solid thud, a spot-on thud,
dead-centre-of-the-ball and cheer-your-lungs-out,
go-down-in-history, kick-of-the-century thud.

A goal! A know-you've-won, a blinder goal. And NOT
a try-again-next-season shot.

Matt Simpson
Liverpool

Billy Jenkins

Billy Jenkins doesn't come to school
every day. He's in a wheelchair.
Sometimes he has to go to the hospital.

He likes football. When the weather's dry
he comes out to support the team.
He wears a tartan rug over his knees.

He lives in the house by the post-box,
the one with the big garden and all the trees.
He sits outside in summer and watches people.

I had a dream about him. It was a Saturday.
Billy Jenkins jumped out of his wheelchair
and ran down the road, kicking a football.

We were all shouting as he passed the full-back
and closed in on the goalie. He scored with ease,
as we waved our tartan rugs in the air.

Tony Charles
Wolverhampton
Wanderers

go Billy!

24

The Penalty

If I place it to his left
    Will he guess wrong?

        If I place it to his right
            Will he guess right?

I'll look to his right
    And place it left

        Or should I look to his left
            And place it right?

No, I'll shape up right
    And hit it right.

        Or should I . . . ?

Ian Blackman
Brighton and Hove Albion

25

Can I av me ball back?

Can I av me ball back
Can I av me ball?
Mister Mister
Chuck it over the wall!

Bouncing off the wall
Bouncing on the floor
Bouncing off the roof
Bouncing on the door
            – oops!

Can I av me ball back
Can I av me ball?
Missis Missis
Chuck it over the wall!

Dodging the washing
Disguising the pass
Sprinting past the shed
Sliding on the grass
              – oops!

26

Can I av me ball back
Can I av me ball?
Mister Mister
Chuck it over the wall!

Storming through the playground
Gliding by the flower bed
Leaping in the corridor
Colliding with the . . . Head!
        – oops!

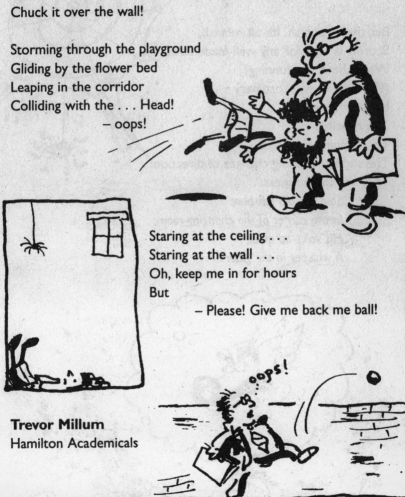

Staring at the ceiling . . .
Staring at the wall . . .
Oh, keep me in for hours
But

        – Please! Give me back me ball!

Trevor Millum
Hamilton Academicals

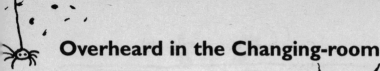

Overheard in the Changing-room

Scoring goals,
That's all they want to hear about!
The swing; the thump;
The leather speeding into the net!

But that's rubbish. It's all rubbish.
Scoring is easy for any well-made boot.
What about the running?
(Oh not like your ordinary
boot or shoe).
The dancing!
The skipping sideways!
The sudden dazzling changes of direction!
They are the business.

> *Said the old left boot*
> *In the corner of the changing-room,*
> *His voice so quiet,*
> *A whisper in the gloom.*

Goals? Nothing! Crash, bang, wallop
And back to the spot.
But the dancing! Imagine.
Tip-tapping the ball,
Inside the foot, outside,
Toecap, instep, heel.
Can you? Can you imagine it?
Swivelling, shuffling,
Not too fast, then checking,
And only then the sudden dash . . .
The sure-footed surge of speed.
Those are the delights:
>   *An old left boot*
>   *Slung in the corner*
>   *Amid the shirts and shorts*
>   *Whispering – 'Goals? Nothing.'*

Although . . .
Although to tap it,
To screw it,
To trickle it,
To slot it,
To slice it,
To lob it,
To swerve it,
To drift it,
To drive it
Past those outstretched hands –
There was pleasure in that.
>   *Last season's boot*
>   *Chucked in the corner,*
>   *Muttering*
>   *Mumbling away.*

Gerard Benson
Arsenal

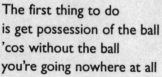

Pre-match Rap

The first thing to do
is get possession of the ball
'cos without the ball
you're going nowhere at all

work it from the back
build it up real slow
no back passing
there's only one way to go

take it down the middle
or send it out wide
just make sure you don't
give it the opposing side

when you get to the box
knock it on through
try to penetrate
with a quick one-two

with close control
work that ball
carry it past
their defensive wall

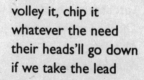

volley it, chip it
whatever the need
their heads'll go down
if we take the lead

give it what you've got
body and soul
whatever you do
just go for goal

and come the final whistle
you'll have the fame you seek
absolute heroes
till the same time next week

now let's get out there and do the business!

Tony Langham
Bolton Wanderers

31

Losing Marker

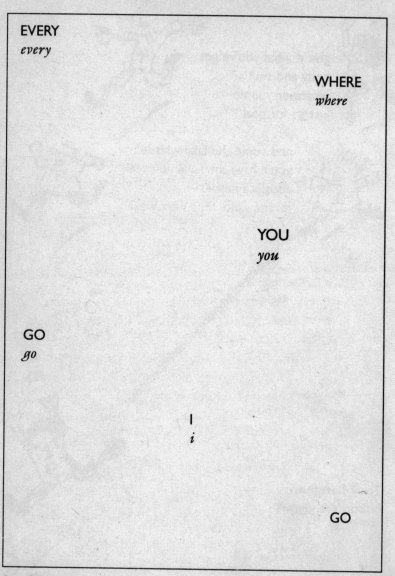

EVERY
every

WHERE
where

YOU
you

GO
go

I
i

GO

Ian Blackman
Brighton and Hove Albion

Substitute

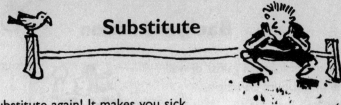

Not substitute again! It makes you sick.
It wouldn't matter if we sometimes won
but we're one down, and taking lots of stick.
It was same last Saturday: 4–1.

Why is it that the Coach will never pick
me for the team? I don't know what I've done.
What's that he's saying now? Go on for Mick
who's hurt his leg? Great! This should be more fun.

The linesman nods: I'm on. I get a kick.
Then Barry passes, Raj goes on a run.
His marker tackles but Raj is too quick:
he floats a lovely ball into the sun.
I head it down. Now – it's just one to one.
And I am past the keeper. Yes! 1–1!

Jill Townsend
Liverpool

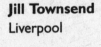

Backyard Kickin

Kickin mi football gainst di wall
mi neighbours complain
but I no harm at all
kickin mi football
dat's all!

Kickin mi football out on di street
me and mi posse we compete
mi neighbours complain
but our answer is sweet
We kickin a football
dat's all!

Dad kick mi football at di weekend
Kickin so hard he pretend
he really de boss o' England!
Mi neighbours complain
they gotta window to mend
cos Dad kick mi football
over di wall.

     Dat's all.

Chris Riley
Italy

Match Report

So there's just ten minutes left
right and Benson says okay you're
on right just like that right no
warning or anything like that and
I say what position sir right and
he says on the right right so I go
on right and as soon as we get
started Degsey bangs one over to me
right and I leg it right down to
the corner flag and knock one over
right and Billy Khan's right there
deadcentre and he hits it just right
and it goes right in sweetasanut

Tony Langham
Bolton Wanderers

35

The Best Match of the Year

Did you see it?
Did *you* see it?

Lee's brilliant shot, from way outside the box:

WOOOSH!

Top left-hand corner of the net;
their goalie had NO CHANCE.

Did you see it?
Did *you* see it?

But what about . . . but what about our keeper's

SUPERSAVE

just before half-time?
Old glue-gloves held on to it.

Did you see it?
Did *you* see it?

Wow! Cor! Phew, I'll never forget those two

CRUNCHING

tackles by Big Chris;
crucial, I mean K-Roo-Shul.

Did you see it?
Did *you* see it?

No, neither did I.

Mike Johnson
Blackburn Rovers

36

Why Groundsmen Never Relax

We're the touchy ones who patch up the pitches
when the action of each game dispatches grass patches
and batches of scratch-marks, where boots catch, carve ditches.
We're grouches because of such hitches.
We've a hotch-potch of blotches, a richness of itches,
much agony, ouches and stitches,
all actually brought on by these glitches
due to passes and tackles and switches.
And it's match-watching which is
what hatches our unnatural twitches.

Nick Toczek
Bradford

The Football Pitch is Waterlogged

The football pitch is waterlogged
the grass is like an ocean.
Because of all the rain and mud
everything's slow motion.

The full-back's wearing flippers
instead of football boots
and tracksuits have been replaced
by frogmen's diving suits.

The wingers have got waders,
the left one — a life jacket
the right one — a red pacamac
from a plastic packet.

The centre-forward's snorkelling
and wearing water-wings.
There are linesmen on the Lilos
and the ref has rubber rings.

The sweeper sails a speedboat
that has a big propeller.
The manager's not managing
to keep up his umbrella.

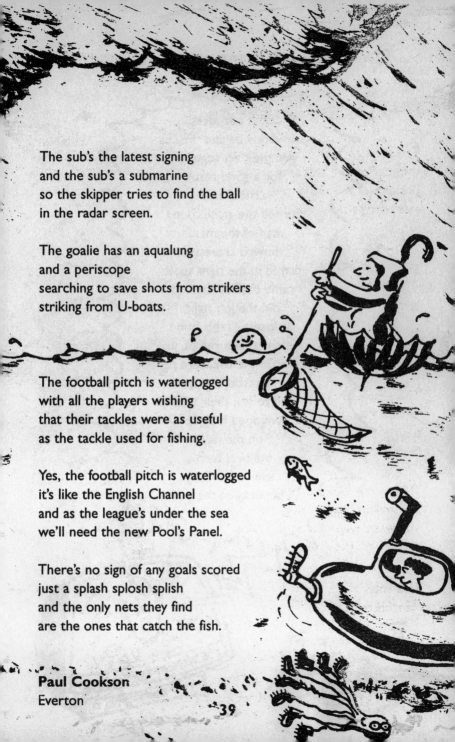

The sub's the latest signing
and the sub's a submarine
so the skipper tries to find the ball
in the radar screen.

The goalie has an aqualung
and a periscope
searching to save shots from strikers
striking from U-boats.

The football pitch is waterlogged
with all the players wishing
that their tackles were as useful
as the tackle used for fishing.

Yes, the football pitch is waterlogged
it's like the English Channel
and as the league's under the sea
we'll need the new Pool's Panel.

There's no sign of any goals scored
just a splash splosh splish
and the only nets they find
are the ones that catch the fish.

Paul Cookson
Everton

39

Football Word Bank

rank outsiders
everybody behind the ball
got their act together
for a good result
crucial save
turned the game round
man of the match
showed character
played in the right spirit
came back at the end
did the job right
no losers in this game
an amazing turnaround
tactics on the day were right
a fantastic triumph
retired to lick their wounds
wrapped it all up
on the day
the best team
came out on top
a bit lucky in the end

Rita Ray
Manchester City

MR. WISE · AFTER · THE · EVENT

Football Story

This is the foot.

This is the foot
That kicked the ball.

This is the foot
That kicked the ball
That scored the goal.

This is the foot
That kicked the ball
That scored the goal
That won the cup.

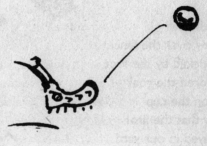

This is the foot
That kicked the ball
That scored the goal
That won the cup
The day that the final
Was played in our yard.

This is the ball.

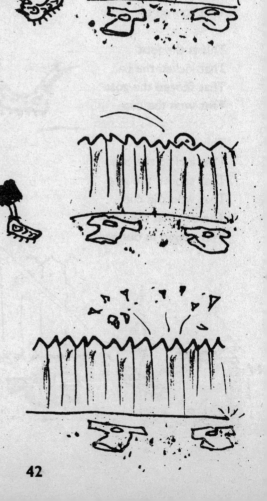

This is the ball
That was kicked by the foot
That scored the goal
That won the cup
The day that the final
Was played in our yard.

This is the ball
That flew over the fence
When kicked by the foot
That scored the goal
That won the cup
The day that the final
Was played in our yard.

This is the ball
That flew over the fence
And smashed the window
Of next-door's kitchen
When kicked by the foot
That scored the goal
That won the cup
The day that the final
Was played in our yard.

This is the boy.

This is the boy
Who ran away.

This is the boy
Who ran away
To hide in the shed
When he heard the crash
Made by the ball
That flew over the fence
And smashed the window
Of next-door's kitchen

When kicked by the foot
That scored the goal
That won the cup
The day that the final
Was played in our yard.

This is the father.

This is the father
Who found the boy
Who ran away
To hide in the shed
When he heard the crash
Made by the ball
That flew over the fence
And smashed the window
Of next-door's kitchen
When kicked by the foot
That scored the goal
That won the cup
The day that the final
Was played in our yard.

This is the father
Who dragged home the boy
Who ran away
When he heard the crash
Made by the ball
That flew over the fence
And smashed the window
Of next-door's kitchen
When kicked by the foot
That scored the goal
That won the cup
The day that the final
Was played in our yard.

44

This is the hand.

This is the hand
Of the father
Who dragged home the boy
Who ran away
When he heard the crash
Made by the ball
That flew over the fence
And smashed the window
Of next-door's kitchen
When kicked by the foot
That scored the goal
That won the cup
The day that the final
Was played in our yard.

This is the hand
Of the father
Who spanked the boy
Who ran away
When he heard the crash
Made by the ball
That flew over the fence
And smashed the window
Of next-door's kitchen
When kicked by the foot
That scored the goal
That won the cup
The day that the final
Was played in our yard.

And this is the boy
Who can't sit down.

John Foster
Carlisle United

Here Are Some Late Football Results

(These matches all kicked off at half past a quarter to)

Back to the Future	3	Batman	2
BBC	2	Channel	4
Who're you waiting	4	Would anyone like an After	8
Frank Bruno hits 'em for	6	Enid Blyton's Famous	5
U	2	Me	2
The Magnificent	7	The Secret	7
Rocky	4	Home Alone	2
All my friends have got	1	I Want one	2
It's Top of the Pops –			
it's This Week's Number	1	Rambo	3
But Mum why do I have	2	Red Dwarf	6
Jaws	5	Wayne's World	2
You're looki-	0	I'm feeli-	0

David Horner
Hull City and Warrington Town

Will it Go to a Replay?

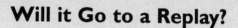

Last night's cup-tie
West Ham and Sheffield United
was so exciting, really tough.

Two teams battled it out
through the rain and mud
as goal after goal
thudded into the net.

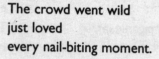

The crowd went wild
just loved
every nail-biting moment.

Four–four
with five minutes left
of extra time
both teams down to nine men
and the tension tightening.

In those dying minutes
both sides
cleared their goal lines
with desperate headers.

West Ham missed a penalty
United missed an open goal.

With seconds to go
a replay at Bramall Lane
seemed certain, until

West Ham had to go in for her tea
and Sheffield United went to the shops
for his mum.

David Harmer
Sheffield United

'Ard 'Ead

A tenacious young striker named 'Nutty' McAull
In training one day was headbutting a wall
When quizzed why he did it
'e said 'Obvious, innit –
I 'ate gettin' 'eadaches from 'eadin' a ball!'

Ian Blackman
Brighton and Hove Albion

Dinner-time

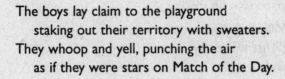

The boys lay claim to the playground
    staking out their territory with sweaters.
They whoop and yell, punching the air
    as if they were stars on Match of the Day.

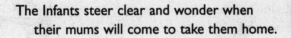

The girls huddle to one side, clapping rhythms,
  skipping rhymes, hop-scotching their time.

Dinner ladies like Sumo wrestlers stand guard.

The Infants steer clear and wonder when
    their mums will come to take them home.

A lone teacher hugs her coffee mug,
    shrugs off the wind and casts a watchful eye.

Other kids gather in corners to swap
    bubble gum cards
        and jokes
           they don't understand.

Pie Corbett
Arsenal

Sideline

Nab that ball!
Steady on!
Don't let Wilson get you down.
Ooooops! That was nasty
– never mind,
it's only mud on your behind.
Come on captain,
make a break
Ouch! * * * * *
Don't start crying for heaven's sake!
It's just a scratch,
that's just a bruise.
We'll treat it later with ice-cubes.
It's only blood that's on your face . . .
Watch out!
Quick, quick, get into place!
Run! Run! Don't stop,
don't look around.
Don't mind that Wilson on the ground.
Kick, quick, kick! kick!
You'll do it yet.
You did! It's in!
It's in the net!
We've won! We've won!
It's all a dream,
and my mum's captain
      of
         the
            team!!!

Una Leavy
Manchester United

Ere We Go

Ere we go
No fear of foe
Football fans
In frost and snow

Football fans
In fire or flood
In gales that blow,
The truest blood.

Support em high
Support em low
Always Yes
And never No
Ere we, ere we, ere we go.

John Kitching
Sheffield Wednesday

Football Facts

Twenty Things Needed for a Game of Football in the Local Park

1   Even number of players with at least four wearing anoraks or duffel-coats.

2   Remove anoraks or duffel-coats to use as goal posts.

3   Pick teams.

4   Do not pick smallest or fattest ones last.

5   Get out ball.

6   Argue with each other as to whose turn it is to bring ball.

7   Borrow friend's bike to go home and fetch ball.

8   Meanwhile practise the art of spitting and clearing nose.

9   Get out ball.

10   Argue with person who got ball as to why ball is flat.

11   Borrow another friend's bike to fetch pump.

12   Meanwhile practise rude words to shout at non-existent referee.

13   Pump up ball.

14   Kick off and start game.

15   Commentate like John Motson on passing movements and eventual shot.

16   Argue whether shot
a) missed
b) went in
c) went over anorak post
d) would have hit post and (i) gone in
(ii) bounced out

17   Try to retrieve ball from muddy ditch behind goals.

18   Do not head ball for at least fifteen minutes.

19   Get jeans as dirty as possible because the dirtier they are the better you must have played.

20   Play until
a) everyone goes home
b) it is too dark to see
c) you are winning
d) you are winning, it is too dark to see and it is your ball anyway so you're going home.

Paul Cookson
Everton

How to Line Up Your Team

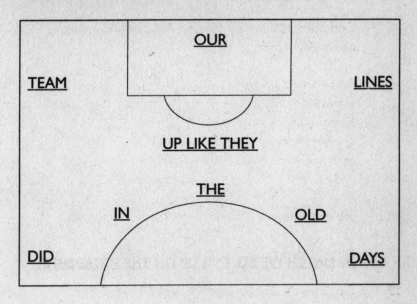

OUR

TEAM   LINES

UP LIKE THEY

THE

IN   OLD

DID   DAYS

FOR
THIS GAME WE ALL
CON CEN TRATE
ON DE FENCE

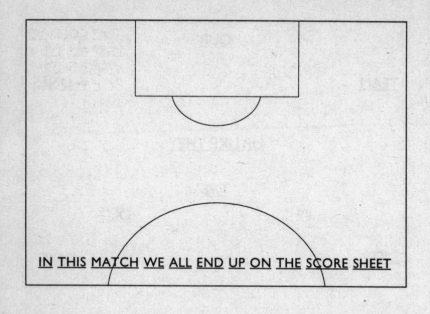

IN THIS MATCH WE ALL END UP ON THE SCORE SHEET

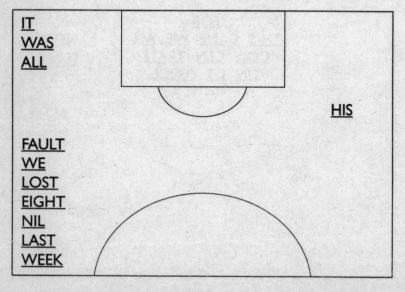

IT
WAS
ALL

HIS

FAULT
WE
LOST
EIGHT
NIL
LAST
WEEK

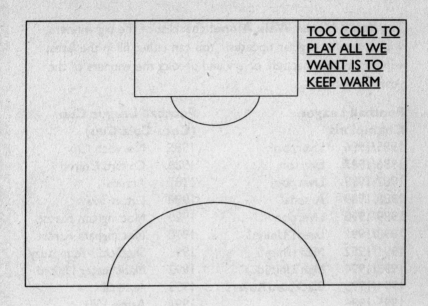

TOO COLD TO
PLAY ALL WE
WANT IS TO
KEEP WARM

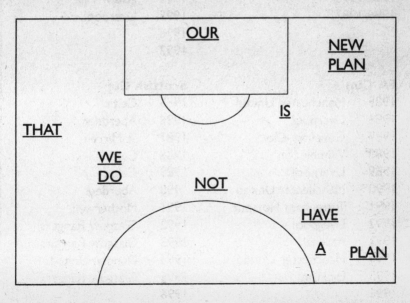

OUR

NEW
PLAN

THAT

IS

WE
DO

NOT

HAVE

A PLAN

John Coldwell Gillingham

61

Winners!

The **You'll Never Walk Alone!** checklist of the big winners, with space for regular updates! You can either fill in the latest winners as they happen, or try and predict the winners of the years to come!

Football League Champions

1985/1986	Liverpool
1986/1987	Everton
1987/1988	Liverpool
1988/1989	Arsenal
1989/1990	Liverpool
1990/1991	Leeds United
1991/1992	Man United
1993/1994	Man United
1994/1995	Blackburn Rovers
1995/1996	
1996/1997	

Football League Cup (Coca-Cola Cup)

1985	Norwich City
1986	Oxford United
1987	Arsenal
1988	Luton Town
1989	Nottingham Forest
1990	Nottingham Forest
1991	Sheffield Wednesday
1992	Manchester United
1993	Arsenal
1994	Aston Villa
1995	Liverpool
1996	
1997	

FA Cup

1985	Manchester United
1986	Liverpool
1987	Coventry City
1988	Wimbledon
1989	Liverpool
1990	Manchester United
1991	Tottenham Hotspur
1992	Liverpool
1993	Arsenal
1994	Manchester United
1995	Everton
1996	
1997	

Scottish Cup

1985	Celtic
1986	Aberdeen
1987	St Mirren
1988	Celtic
1989	Celtic
1990	Aberdeen
1991	Motherwell
1992	Glasgow Rangers
1993	Glasgow Rangers
1994	Dundee United
1995	Glasgow Rangers
1996	
1997	

Scottish League Champions

1985/1986	Celtic
1986/1987	Glasgow Rangers
1987/1988	Celtic
1988/1989	Glasgow Rangers
1989/1990	Glasgow Rangers
1990/1991	Glasgow Rangers
1991/1992	Glasgow Rangers
1993/1994	Glasgow Rangers
1994/1995	Glasgow Rangers
1995/1996	
1996/1997	

Scottish League Cup

1985/1986	Aberdeen
1986/1987	Glasgow Rangers
1987/1988	Glasgow Rangers
1988/1989	Glasgow Rangers
1989/1990	Aberdeen
1990/1991	Glasgow Rangers
1991/1992	Hibernian
1993/1994	Glasgow Rangers
1994/1995	Glasgow Rangers
1995/1996	
1996/1997	

European Cup

1985	Juventus
1986	Steaua Bucharest
1987	Porto
1988	PSV Eindhoven
1989	AC Milan
1990	AC Milan
1991	Red Star Belgrade
1992	Barcelona
1993	Marseille
1994	AC Milan
1995	Ajax
1996	
1997	

World Cup

1958	Brazil
1962	Brazil
1966	England
1970	Brazil
1974	West Germany
1978	Argentina
1982	Italy
1986	Argentina
1990	West Germany
1994	Brazil
1998	

European Cup Winners' Cup

1985	Everton
1986	Dynamo Kiev
1987	Ajax
1988	Mechelen
1989	Barcelona
1990	Sampdoria
1991	Manchester United
1992	Werder Bremen
1993	Parma
1994	Arsenal
1995	Real Zaragoza
1996	
1997	

'ERE WE GO! Macmillan £2.99

Football poems compiled by David Orme, with football facts by Ian Blackman, and illustrations by Marc Vyvyan-Jones.

Football Mad

Gizza go of yer footie,
Just one belt of the ball?
Lend yer me scarf on Satdee
for just one boot at the wall?

Give yer a poster of Gazza
for one tiny kick with me right?
Do y' after be that mingey?
Go on, don't be tight!

A chest-it-down to me left foot,
a touch, a header, a dribble?
A shot between the goalie's legs,
a pass right down the middle?

Y' can borree me Madonna records
for as long as ever y' like,
I'll give yer a go around the block
on me brandnew mountain bike.

One day I'll be playin' for Liverpule
wen Yooze are all forgot:
go on, a titchy kick of yer footie,
one meezly penulty shot?

I'll get yer a season ticket
when I am in THE TEAM,
and wen I'm scorin' in the Cup
you'll be sittin' by the Queen.

Matt Simpson

The first of David Orme's fabulous collections of poems about the one thing guaranteed to interest 99 per cent of normal human beings . . . FOOTBALL!